A GUIDE FOR YOUR DATING JOURNEY

TaSheekia Harris

Contact Information:

Tasheekia Harris

Phone: 1-888-364-0002

Email: cdfs2006@yahoo.com

Website Address: www.cdfs2006.com

Publication:

ISBN: 978-0-9753857-1-5

Printed in the United States of America First Edition Printing: February 2021©

Sozo Omnimedia

Content editing by: Danielle Viens-Payne Author's Photo by: Nyla Damico, Nyla D. Photography

Book layout by: Samuel Okike (Psalmyy on Fiverr).

Acknowledgments

For my son, Jaden Perry, who gave me the strength, motivation, and courage to keep my focus as a mother, and for sharing me with the world.

For my bonus children: I am delighted to be a part of your lives, and I look forward to many joy-filled years together.

For my husband, Walter Harris, showed me that love can be genuine and enjoyable.

To my parents, Charlie McCormick, Kenny, and Sheila Edwards: You have each shown me what sacrifice entails, have offered a lifetime of wisdom nuggets, and have been genuine models of the true meaning of family.

For my "Girls", which includes amazing young ladies who have participated in the Crowning Daughters for Success Enrichment Program, and those who have read the *Dressing My Inner Beauty Journal* (authored by me): I had each of you in mind throughout my "single life" journey. I did not settle because I knew you were watching me. My prayer is that I make each of you proud.

Foreword

I cannot express enough my excitement to write this foreword for my lovely wife, who is also my best friend. I will forever remember the moment we first met. What was supposed to be just a short lunch meet-up turned into hours and hours of purpose and connection. When I grabbed her hand, things changed, and God gripped our lives together, and we walked on the same path for a common course. She became the breath of fresh air I needed, and we debunked the normal process of dating. Many women undermine their true value when there is so much wealth lying dormant and unseen. Similar to a pearl, she must understand and see herself as a gift that brings value to the one who is willing to pay the cost. Get ready to take your journey with Tasheekia as she gives you honest, authentic, and empowering tools taken directly out of our dating relationship and her own experiences. It is a guarantee that you will not only be empowered, but you will have a desire to want more from the beginning to the end.

Walt Harris

Former NFL/Speaker/Philanthropist

Table of Contents

Hey! Hey! Hey!

My P.Y.P. Ladies,

I am so excited to (indirectly) be on this dating journey with you. This guide will make a positive impact on your dating life—whether now or later. Let me start by clearing up a few things. As I pondered writing this guide, I considered how strategic, wise, and intentional a girl must be in the dating world. While desiring the optimum dating experiences for myself, it was imperative to my soul, ministry, and everything that pertains to me that I dated productively. Before you advance in reading this text, I would like to make some necessary clarifications.

- I am not here to make any judgments.
- You do not have to mimic my life to date effectively.
- I do not know it all, but God has given me some very impactful nuggets.
- You can do everything right, and *he* can still be the wrong one.
- The content I provide is not to control you but to empower you.

However, I am confident that the *Lived Experiences*, *Pearl Moments*, *Affirmations*, *Reflections*, and *Pearls of Wisdom* sections implemented within this guide will give you the **confidence** to never equate your worth with being paired with a man, the **courage** to not shadow the superficial dating goals promoted throughout the media, the **character** to set Godly standards as you date and wait for your one true love, and the **faith** to delight in the Lord as He prepares, equips and guides two souls together as one.

When I think of a pearl's experience, I compare it to the human experience. The pearl's process reveals just how God uses irritants in our lives, not to demean us, but to add value as we surrender to His will. Yes! As exasperating as it can be to experience disappointment, challenges, and the whirlwinds of dating, the inestimable happens when we are faithful, obedient, and ever-evolving despite romance flames or fails. Just as that irritant-type substance, the grit contributes to the oyster's ability to protect itself, and eventually secretes a fluid that layers the irritant until the most unique gemstone is created—the pearl. Of all the gems, the pearl is the only one formed and found in a living creature. The pearl is also the only gem that is naturally spectacular, which is unlike the diamond, ruby, and other jewels that require cutting or polishing before use.

Time for Comparison

Just as the pearl is produced from an irritant, so are we. Think of a situation that should have demolished you, but polished you.

Just as the pearl is rare and intricately created, so are we. Look at your fingerprints. There are none like it in all the world.

Just as the pearl's value will never decrease, neither will ours. Allow the Word to be your source. It declares that we are so valuable that God limited His power, lowered Himself, and lived among His creation because we are His precious Pearls. Look no further; you are the Pearl!

- Your mind is the seat of your choices, and Scripture declares that *whatsoever a man thinks so is he*. Protect it, because it is your Pearl.
- Your children (if you have any) are unique gifts from God. Protect them; they are your Pearls.
- Your testimony is a personal, significant experience that gives God glory. It empowers and challenges others and infuses growth. Protect it, because it is your Pearl.
- Your vagina is powerful—more powerful than keeping a man. Protect it. It is your Pearl.
- Your soul is eternal. When life on earth is no more, the soul will live in eternity with God or separate from Him. Protect it, because it is your Pearl.
- You can never recapture a single second that has passed. Time cannot be duplicated, put on hold, or replaced. Protect it, because it is your Pearl.
- Your gifts and talents are blessings to empower and inspire others on life's journey. Protect them; they are your Pearls.
- If the oyster was created to protect the natural pearl, you have all you need in Christ to **Protect Your Pearls**!

You will never look at a string of pearls the same again! Each time you see or wear them, they will symbolize the invisible string of jewels—created perfectly and exceptionally—that make up the woman you are; and Christ is the clamp that holds them all together.

My Prayer for You

If you are reading this guide, 9 times out of 10 you are single, or you understand that no matter your relationship status, it is your responsibility to perform due diligence and take care of the sacred valuables that make up your existence. It is my hope that by now you have come into the knowledge of how special, rare, and valuable you are. Just you! All things gain value because of you. Yes! *You* make the difference, and without you, there would be a great loss.

Let us pray!

Abba, our redeemer, and strength, we exalt you because of who you are, and thank you for the amazing things you have done. You have been faithful during times of our unfaithfulness. There is no one else we proclaim as Lord other than the name of Jesus.

I come into agreement with my dear sisters who are reading this guide—that you will demonstrate your faithfulness and power in their lives. I ask that you bring comfort, resilience, and anointed ease into their dating experiences. I beseech you to reroute and move in a different direction, every distractive spirit that comes in the form of companionship, help, or love. Build my sisters so strongly that they discern the wrong person at the sight of him.

Dismantle every evil prayer that prevents her from a productive relationship that could result in a lasting marriage. Destroy every generational curse sent through her bloodline that blocks her husband from finding her. Open her heart to first forgive herself, and then to forgive anyone who has offended, disappointed, and hurt her. Let every act of evil that has limited her begin to work for her good. Allow her to be content in all things because you are with her. Bring restoration, rejuvenation and align her with your Holy Word.

Your Word declares that when we delight in you, you will give us the desires of our hearts. Let her be so into you that your timing will be sufficient, and your presence will keep her from desperately embracing those you have not sent. As her future husband is praying for his wife, prepare them both. Let them not pass each other by, but give them divine timing, the perfect place, and an anointed connection. Make all demonic, relational breeches, barriers, and sabotage completely powerless.

I come into agreement with your Word that declares that it is not good for man to be alone. I pray that you anoint the content of this guide to encourage, empower and equip her for the *one*. I declare all counterfeits will be exposed! Give her the appropriate accountability partners that will circle her with intercession, Godly advice, and authentic friendship.

In Jesus' name. Amen.

Pearl Moment:

A MIXTURE OF FAITH AND WORKS WILL MANIFEST THE IMPOSSIBLE.

T. HARRIS

A Letter of Commitment to Self

The Bible tells us in James 2:17 that *faith without works is dead.* Use the space provided below to write a commitment plan. I suggest you start with one of the most powerful healing agents—an apology to yourself. If you have neglected your Pearls, have allowed others to trample over or misuse your Pearls, or have been ashamed of your Pearls, acknowledge it and forgive.

In great detail, map out your commitment to Protecting Your Pearls, and list ways in which you will be intentional. Be mindful of those with whom you share your Pearls!

Pearls of Wisdom

The scriptural references below are biblical principles that disclose the importance of having a "made-up mind" and a committed heart. As you date (or wait) consistently check your inner-commitment radar, as it is the key to success and will cancel out indecisiveness. Any doubt in what God can do will cripple your faith, obedience, and commitment.

- James 1:6-9 - *But let him ask in faith, with no doubting, for he who doubts is like a wave of the sea driven and tossed by the wind.*
- Matthew 6:24 - *No one can serve two masters; for either he will hate the one and love the other, or else he will be loyal to one and despise the other. You cannot serve God and mammon.*
- Galatians 5:7-8 - *You ran well; Who hindered you from obeying the truth? This persuasion does not come from Him who calls you.*
- Esther 4:16 - *Go, gather all the Jews who are present in Shushan, and fast for me; neither eat nor drink for three days, night or day. My maids and I will fast likewise. And so I will go before the king, which is against the law, and if I perish, I perish!*

Pearl Reflection

Who is responsible for your peace as you date (or wait), and why?

If your dating experience does not align with your expectations, what are some steps that you can take to resolve the matter?

What dating strategies are you prepared to implement to Protect Your Pearls?

Pearl Affirmation:

MY COMMITMENT TO GOD AND MYSELF WILL NEVER WAVER DUE TO A LACK OF LOYALTY FROM ANOTHER PERSON.

Pearl Moment:

A *WHOLE* WOMAN IS COMPLETE WITH OR WITHOUT HIM, BUT NOT WITHOUT *HIM*.

T. HARRIS

A Lived Experience: Whole and Ready

Wholeness is a very intrinsic aspect of self. Many women draw from brokenness and find it exceedingly difficult to discern what space to give a man who seeks to connect with her.

My dating life began at 15 years old, according to my mom. The only clue I had about dating was derived from my favorite songs, entertainers, and friends. This lack of knowledge caused me to "struggle date" because I did not have a solid foundation. Can you relate? Imagine if you had a healthy dating experience from the beginning. It could have eliminated so much.

From a teenager to adulthood, I participated in adult activities but had the maturity of a child. One of the worst times to allow someone into your sacred dating space is when you are broken, confused, and have yet to discern your worth. Dang! This is the very opposite of what I did when I dated in my adolescent years.

For some reason, right after a failed relationship, someone was happy that the person I was dating messed up. I also thought it was a blessing because of the saying, "What you do not want, someone else will gladly take care of."

Unfortunately, I did not take care of *myself*. My value system consisted of tangible items that were given to me. Broken, I believed the "girlfriend" title would fix me, boost me, and give me what I needed to feel accepted. That mindset landed me in environments to attract men just like me—broken. So, I began a destructive pattern that continued along my dating journey; I consistently replaced people, but without changing my mindset.

I received Christ at the age of 25, and over the last 20 years, my greatest ponderance has been: *If only I knew when I was younger, what I know now!* I think many of us could give our younger selves some proper advice.

Let us continue with my journey experience to wholeness. I got married the same year I received Christ. We were incredibly good friends, and we both loved God and desired to do things according to the principles of the Bible. We were two *healed* people who blamed each other for not being what each of us needed to fill the holes in our souls. I was married for 11 years and was blessed with a handsome, healthy baby. No sooner than our son could walk, the marriage ended.

However, *I* could not end! I refused to do life the same way I had done it in the years before salvation. Fortunately, I could not afford to date the same way. I came into an awareness of my string of Pearls, which represents what God entrusts in me. It allows me to be authentic and has helped me to empower others.

Daily, as I looked at myself in the mirror, I realized that the Pearl was me and that everything I encountered would gain value just by being attached to me. It was as clear as day. I heard a still, quiet voice say, "You must protect what is valuable. You have protected invaluable things for too long. It is time to use the tools I have given you to protect *you*."

Arriving at wholeness was the fundamental experience that unlocked my readiness. If I was to have a dissimilar dating adventure than those of my past, I had to become pliable by the Word of God. I shunned everything that unsettled my wholeness or gave me a false sense of freedom, hope, or happiness. Yes! It was way different and very new to me. For the first time since the age of 15, I was open to a new idea of being loved. I was not moved by which guy was next on the dating wheel because Jesus—Yeshua, the Alpha, and Omega—was on guard, and each guy would have to get through him to get to me. I was available in the sense of not being with anyone, but I was not easily accessible.

I used to ask for healing. I thought that once the pain was gone, I was free to move on. Healing is only the start; wholeness will thrust you to the finish. At the cessation of my first marriage, I had over 11 years of ministry experience, oppositions, triumphs, fallacies, and tears of joy and pain. Forgiveness through it all brought refreshing healing that I could not describe even if I had a million years to explain it. Healing decreased pain, and even shame, but I continued to seek, bond, and build my personal relationship with Jesus, which truly made me whole. Had I settled for healing alone, I would have missed one of the greatest processes that would open me up for wholeness.

I remember thinking, "It's another failed relationship." I started to feel worse because of the broken covenant and knowing I was single again at the age of 37. I felt alone, incomplete, and like a total failure because I listened to the enemy for one second too long. This one life event, a divorce, almost caused me to forfeit the millions of "why's" I already had to move forward.

One of my most pivotal prayers was: "Lord, I am going to be alone!"

I can still hear the Holy Spirit's response. "You are speaking from a place of healing. If you knew the power of my presence, you would not dare conclude that you are alone just because one person chose a different path that did not include you."

Yikes! I was so ashamed and quickly became remorseful. How could I undermine the presence of God? How could I compare the presence of a person to the presence of my God? Healing from my divorce caused me to feel better again, but wholeness allowed me to forge ahead. I began to think about the ten lepers in the book of Matthew. They called out to Jesus for help, and he graciously healed them, but only one returned to say, "thank you".

Healed: the process of becoming sound or healthy again.

Leprosy brings pain; it is infectious, and amongst the symptoms are sores and the possible loss of body parts. Subsequently, the nine who were healed and did not return to thank him no longer experienced leprosy, but the scars (the effects on the mind and body) were still there. The act of receiving but not caring enough to pursue the one who healed them leaves one to conclude that they needed something from Jesus but expressed no desire for Jesus himself. So, they left with healing, but without understanding that they needed the healer to be whole. God not only wanted to free them from their issues; He also desired to destroy the side effects.

When the one returned and thanked him, Jesus asked, "Were not all ten cleansed? Where are the nine?" Ten had asked and received, but one desired *more*. Ten had confidence that Jesus could, but the one believed there was *more*. Ten went on their way to show themselves to the priest as they were commanded by Jesus, but the one did not want the approval of man or the mere cleansing of his body. He knew that if Jesus could heal him, he could also make him whole. Healing set the ten free from some things, but wholeness gave the one power.

All I can say is that I have seen many people healed. Jesus noticeably met their desires, and they left him just as the nine lepers had, and missed out on a bigger blessing.

Let this marinate in your spirit. If you believe God can heal or deliver you from alcoholism, you will be freed from the desire to drink, but your lack of wholeness will cause you to replace alcohol with another debilitating habit. When the woman at the well was made whole in the book of John, Jesus knew the relationship between them would eliminate her thirst for the men who dehydrated her spirit and would instead give her a thirst for him. A woman healed from a past relationship will replace her ex-lover with a new one, but he will have the same spirit as the old. A *whole* woman loses all attraction to that which undermines her value, her call, and her God.

Now, I was whole, but my readiness was a process. During my single years, wholeness gave me the peace, willingness, and patience to allow God to guide my dating experiences. I dated, and I cared for them, but wholeness would not let me settle. I refused to go through it on my own or to be right only within myself. So, after dating for a little while, I stopped dating altogether. My grandmother joked, "Girl, how is a man going to find you?"

If any man could find me, I would know for sure that he had been searching because I was not on display. I was where they keep the most expensive jewels—in the far back, and within the safe.

All along, God was getting me ready. Do not allow the length of your single season to provoke you, nor make you believe that you will remain single. Wholeness did not give me a pass for the work that needed to be done. Each person's workload to becoming ready is different. I had a lot of work to do, many experiences to take on, and a son who did not need a man to occupy his mom's attention. When I achieved what was required of me, God led my now-husband, Walt, into the safe.

At the time, I had an incredibly unique way of thinking—a *whole* way of thinking—that totally baffled me but tested his sincerity. Walt could see the difference I made in the lives of others and was very inspired. He reached out to me and said that if I ever offered empowerment sessions in his area to please let him know. It was a very innocent approach, and I was wonderfully comfortable with it.

We conversed over the phone for a few months before I was in his neck of the woods to implement an empowerment program for girls. I decided to have lunch with him as I waited for a friend to arrive. Astonishingly, traffic dilemmas postponed her for five hours. So, he and I laughed, talked, walked, and talked some more. He even held my hand. I felt a very genuine connection and would later discover that he was having a similar experience.

Lunch was over, but we continued to talk as I traveled to my destination. He shared his desire to see me again. My wholeness was able to perceive that it was not what he needed at all.

Although I also desired to see him, I knew that my assignment was to pour into him from a genuine place. So, I had to put the tingly feelings aside to be who he needed, and not who he wanted. I was able to recognize his brokenness and was bold enough to speak what God inspired me to say without fear of rejection.

I agreed to converse with him once I left, but I had settled on not dating nor seeing him again until God approved. Wholeness gave me the power, courage, and confidence to do something different. We became the best of phone friends as we removed the pressures of dating from the beginning.

"Just be you," I shared. I sensed a call on his life, but I also sensed a compromise due to condemnation. I noticed the healing virtue of God upon his countenance, but some messes needed to be cleaned up.

After some time, we decided to spiritually date. We prayed, conversed a lot, and established a very divine, spiritual connection that was unbelievably strong. I was his spiritual girlfriend. (LOL!) He later asked if he could come to see me, but I knew he was not ready. "Not now" was my answer.

Fast forward five months to when I heard Holy Spirit say, "He's ready. You can see him." In that time, his spirit man had grown so beautifully! I was amazed by how much he had yielded to God—not to please me, but to locate the person he thought he could never be again. My lack of distractions and ability to see the ultimate ending (which may not have included *us*) allowed that moment to transpire and resulted in his reconnection to God.

My heart fluttered, but prior to that moment, I did not care if I saw him, or if God had given me a "no". However, I was relieved when God issued a "you can see him" release! When we saw each other, the same connection we experienced five months prior was present, but we still did not start dating. He continued to blossom spiritually right before my eyes. He shared how the pureness of our relationship reminded him of what he had with God before life hit hard. I could discern his wholeness as he spoke about forgiving himself and others, and desiring God above all. After a long heart-to-heart, I suggested that he fast for clarity, direction, and to hear the wisdom of God; and he humbly agreed. After his fast, he said, "I am ready. I need to see you again."

I had felt spiritual compatibility long before, but his wholeness did not mean he was ready. I prayed, and God gave me peace and confirmation. A sister-friend of mine confirmed my release through what God showed her, and it opened me up to another, "Yes, I will see you again." (It is imperative to have strong friends with Godly perspectives.)

I am sure your question is: "I understand him being whole, but how did you know he was ready?"

I knew he was ready when he was whole enough to be totally transparent and gave me the power of choice—to stay or leave. I knew he was ready when he was humble enough to listen, but strong enough to lead. I knew he was ready after many confirmations, but the greatest of all was how he reminded me of the one leper who did not just want Jesus for a blessing; he wanted Jesus because he could not do life without him. We were whole and ready together. This did not create a false sense of perfection. It was a most appreciated green light!

Pearls of Wisdom

The scriptural references below are biblical principles that disclose the importance of having an authentic relationship with God—not just as your blesser, but also as your Savior. Genuine dependency on God yields wholeness, confirms readiness, ensures His everlasting presence, and provides consultation.

- I Samuel 30:8 - *David inquired of the Lord if he should pursue the raiders that attacked his city and took the children and the men. And he answered him, "Pursue for you shall surely overtake them, and without fail recover all."*
- Luke 17:19 - *And He said unto him (the leper), "Arise, go your way. Your faith has made you well."*
- I Corinthians 3:2 - *I fed you with milk and not solid food; for until now you were not able to receive it, and even now you are still not able.*
- I Corinthians 1:29-30 - *…that no flesh should glory in His presence. But of Him, you are in Christ Jesus, who became for us the wisdom of God-and righteousness and sanctification and redemption…*

Pearl Reflection

Use the space below to reflect on the "Whole & Ready" topic. Explain how you will use this information to Protect Your Pearls.

Pearl Affirmation:

I AM WHO GOD SAYS I AM.
I AM NOT DEFINED BY
ANYTHING OUTSIDE OF
WHAT GOD HAS
DECLARED OVER ME!

Pearl Moment:

GOD IS SUCH A GENTLEMAN; HE DOES NOT FORCE HIS WAY IN. HE GIVES US THE CHOICE TO ALLOW HIM IN.

T. HARRIS

A Lived Experience: The Invite

B before you proceed, think of the most prized invitation you have ever received. Who sent it? What preparations did you make to ensure you were in attendance? Do you remember how honored you were to attend and support?

Most of us enjoy being a part of productive, heartfelt occasions. Invites to someone's graduation, retirement celebration, wedding, or any grand initiative are treasures; and they add a sense of inclusion to our lives. Individuals who host events and celebrations are likely to issue a "by invite only" request.

Functions that are "by invite only":

- gives the host the opportunity to personalize the guest list.
- allows the host to create space and opportunities for diversity among guests.
- reveals that invited guests are a priority.

- ensures appropriate accommodations for invitees.

Although it was over 25 years ago, I remember high school graduation like it was yesterday. My grandmother, Pearl, was adamant about receiving an invite. At the time, I did not understand the value of an invite, or how much it triggers feelings of acceptance as invitees bask in the opportunity to celebrate others.

So, yes! I procrastinated, and my grandmother gave me quite the call. I can still hear her voice so vividly, "TASHEEKIA! You are in the doghouse with grandmama!"

She went on to share that she had not received her invitation, and that she would not be attending my graduation without one. Naturally, I had a reply, and shared, "Granny, I told you about graduation over two months ago."

"Ha!" She responded that a *verbal* was tacky for such an occasion, and if I wanted her to be in attendance, she had better receive an invite within enough time to RSVP.

It does not matter how much our world advances; some acts will remain the proper way of doing things. So, yes! I got an invite to my grandma, got out of the doghouse, and she attended my graduation.

I had undermined the power of the invite. Nonetheless, we all want to invite individuals who have our best interest at heart—those who desire to celebrate our accomplishments or initiatives, and those who would support our endeavors with their talent resources or time. You would never invite your worst enemy to a housewarming celebration. You would feel uncomfortable the entire time!

Millions of invites are sent out daily with hopes of someone accepting them. When I receive a *yes* from an invitee, it gives me a warm, fuzzy feeling.

As we dated, "the invite" was an incredibly special topic for me and Walt. Of all the people we could have invited on our dating journey, the most important was the Holy Spirit. Had I known that He was the coolest company, I would have invited him to date with me years before. His presence was imperative to our designment, willpower, and direction. We created this invite without full knowledge of our relationship's outcome.

Imagine if the person whose smile, presence, and genuine intention to celebrate you was able to be a part of all your special moments. That is the feeling—a million times over actually—you will get when you invite God into every aspect of your life, dating and beyond. His Spirit brought the gift of peace, deliverance, sustainability, unlimited favor, and an unmerited amount of joy. I could write pages upon pages and share how vital it was to our ultimate victory that God was always there. The peace was literally beyond our understanding!

Many things outside of us attempted to rattle our relationship, but God's presence kept us constant. The aggravations of life that manifested to regress us, literally progressed our love, commitment and desire to be together. We understood from the beginning that inviting the Holy Spirit would entail honoring His presence, embracing His authority, and flowing with His process no matter how fast or slow it may have seemed. Every time we saw each other, God would wink at us through various situations, signs, and confirmations. We would talk about something, and the very topic would manifest in a sermon, song, or even on a billboard.

The greatest advice I can give is to not wait until a mess appears to invite Him. Yes, He will always come to our aid because He is so faithful to us; but if we would invite him *before* the mess, we may just avoid the mess.

Secondly, if only one person invites Him into the relationship, it will be extremely awkward. Therefore, it is best to understand where individuals stand spiritually before the attachment is sealed. The Bible tells us that when we receive Jesus as our Lord and Savior, the Holy Spirit comes upon us and gives us power. This power saturates us whether we are together or apart. It will take more than five-star dining, laughs, and material things to experience a productive dating relationship. You will need the power to Protect Your Pearls!

I did not know this type of power existed. From my experience, I can warn you that you must learn to be okay when His presence changes things around. You must be okay when His presence challenges you to step up and line up according to your immeasurable worth. You must be okay when His presence drives away the one you love—one who would also crash your life's party without God's interference. Be forewarned that inviting Him will cause others to not show up or reject your invite.

From day to day, when we would invite the Holy Spirit, value was added to our relationship, we had unlimited coaching access, and there was room for deliverance and breakthroughs. We made a deal (which we keep to this day) that we would not go anywhere without Him, and that He has permission to approve or disapprove anything connected to our journey.

Many individuals only invite Him as a cleanup service. It's hilarious! We shun His authority when we assume we know it all; but when the mess appears, we want Him to clean it up. Much of the mess that accumulates is due to poor planning, choices, a lack of Godly presence, and giving the wrong people invites into the relationship.

It became our custom to invite Him in every morning with a "good morning prayer" via text, FaceTime, or phone call. We asked Him to be a part of our relationship because our experiences taught us that He knew best.

Of all the celebrated milestones and countless causes, many will receive special invites to attend, having the Creator accept the invitation to take part in your daily endeavors is epic. He does not accept the invite because we are so worthy, but because He loves us and desires to assist us on life's journey.

Pearls of Wisdom

The scriptural references below are biblical principles that disclose the importance of the inclusion of the Holy Spirit. He must be top invitee! His Word accompanies Him and guides us with wisdom, knowledge, and understanding. As a result, we walk in righteous determinations as we date or wait.

- Revelations 3:20 - *Behold, I stand at the door, and knock. If anyone should hear my voice and open the door, I will come into him and dine with him, and he with me.*

  This principle is applicable in every aspect of life. The all-powerful God desires to have access to His creation.

- Proverbs 3:6 - *In all your ways acknowledge Him, And He will make your path straight.*

  When we recognize our need for Him, He assists, directs, and empowers us to ensure a successful outcome.

- Psalm 42:1 - *As the dear pants for the water brooks, So my soul pants for you, God.*

  When we long for Him, seek Him, and invite Him into every crevice of our lives, it demonstrates our humility and proves that we take delight in Him. This gives Him the opportunity to reveal His love and fill us with His presence, as well as grants Him instant access to do above and beyond what our minds can imagine.

- Psalm 119:11 - *Your word have I hidden in heart, That I might not sin against You.*

  When God becomes the top invitee, His words accompany Him to give us the wisdom, knowledge, and understanding we need to walk in righteous determinations.

Pearl Reflection

Use the space below to reflect on the "Invite Only" topic. Explain how you will use this information to Protect Your Pearls.

Pearl Affirmation:

I AM SURE OF WHO *I* AM, BUT I WILL INVITE THE ADVISABILITY OF GOD TO SHOW ME WHO *HE* IS.

Pearl Moment:

APPLY LESS PRESSURE SO THAT HE CAN BE HIS AUTHENTIC SELF.

T. HARRIS

A Lived Experience: The No-Pressure Zone

The notion that pressure will burst a pipe is quite common. When water pipes burst, frozen water inside of them completely fills the space and causes an increase in pressure. The pipes cannot contain the pressure, so they burst.

Pressure can bring out a person's best or worst. The San Francisco 49ers defenseman, Lyman Gary Johnson, made that statement in 1985 when he referred to applying pressure to the opposing team's quarterback.

Sometimes we use an enormous amount of pressure to make relationships work because we desire the title over peace and authentic love. There is a self-derived pressure that manifests due to fear of being alone, coveting another person's relationship, or not living up to the relational status quo. This type of pressure causes many women to settle for crumbs when they deserve the entire cake.

It is imperative to avoid pressuring others—like Lyman Johnson strategized and implemented pressure on the quarterback to prevent the touchdown. There is a diabolical pressure that causes many relationships to become superficial. I genuinely believe that pressured love is not love at all.

As Walt and I enjoyed our conversations, I felt compelled to tell him that I wanted us to have a pressure-free experience. Now, I am very territorial, so that was definitely a "Did I just say that?" moment, but I had to own it. We naturally want to control the narrative, so it was not as easy as it sounds. However, as I mentioned previously, I could not afford to date in the same way.

He released a sound of relief, shock, and happiness all at the same time. We both agreed that if we were going to have a genuine relationship, it would be pressure-free so that we could experience each other's authentic selves. "Let's just *be*" was one of our favorite lines. It was not to evade commitment; it was to ensure that any level of commitment was sincere. We had invited the Holy Spirit in, so it was amazingly easy to just be who we needed to be for each other. We did not know how things would end, but the absence of pressure made it an enjoyable experience.

I believe pressure in relational journeys ruins authentic desire and opportunities for individuals to navigate intentionally. Because of our humanity, we can all use innocent reminders from time to time, but the moment we become overbearing, controlling, and manipulative, we jeopardize authenticity.

For example, "I thought you said you were going to call me back" would nudge him to return your call from a place of pressure, and not from his genuine desire to talk to you.

The pressure of "We have been talking long enough; what are we?" pressures the couple to create a title, but not a commitment.

Sexual intimacy is one of the greatest unspoken pressures. Attitudes change, the pressure gets applied, and eyes begin to roll! Sexual intimacy applies pressure because whenever intimacy occurs, oneness manifests, sacredness is tainted, and sometimes women conclude that it is only fair for a couple's journey to begin. When sex (and other exchanges that should be kept for husbands and wives) is implemented in dating experiences, many women get caught up in the role of a wife, but without the title. The pressure is consuming, and either the man will give in just to obtain more benefits or will leave because he is overwhelmed.

I remember when Walt was supposed to call me back, but it got so late that I went to sleep. He called me the next day to explain, and I stopped him. I wanted him to know that it was okay, and there was no pressure. I genuinely understood, and we continued our conversation. The absence of pressure allowed us to see just how much we wanted each other without ultimatums, threats, or manipulation. The lack of pressure did not mean that I had no expectations. A man's relationship with God, his character, and his humility were my top three. Oh, and let us not forget that he had to be funny. Each trait had to be a part of his character just to build a friendship, let alone a relationship.

I did not have to apply pressure to discern the above. Time, observation, and conversation gave me much-needed insight. If you must pressure a man to be a quality person, he will go through the motions until he gets what he wants, and then he will show his true self again. As a preacher, I could have given scripture tests, prayer auditions, and noted church attendance. This type of pressure would have created smokescreens of the guy I desired, but when the pressure expands, things get shady.

There was no pressure to converse daily, date exclusively, or create false hype to please others, which gave us both a sense of freedom, healthy boundaries, and pure motives. I did not have to pressure him to do anything, and that gave me a sense of comfort and peace. When we started to see each other frequently, the desire to be celibate was mutual—no pressure, no manipulation. When we fell in love, it was easy to embrace because there was no pressure and no manipulation. When he said, "I am going to marry you," even though I chuckled, I believed him because there was no pressure and no manipulation.

If you read the book of Judges, you will notice how Delilah applied demonic pressure on Sampson because she was desperate for something to take back to his enemies. Her ultimate desire was not the man himself; she desired personal power, position, and his anointing. Her constant burden to pull something from him, which he did not desire to give her, eventually weakened him, clouded his judgment, and ultimately cost him everything.

We must be incredibly careful to avoid applying manipulative pressure to gain extrinsic exchange for no intrinsic value. I discerned the anointing on Walt's life the first time I looked into his eyes; it would have been iniquitous to pressure him to commit when I realized he was not ready. Instead, we applied pressure to more important things. We focused on our prayer life, building each other up, and we placed consistent pressure on every contrary spirit. Great victories were our portion because of our genuine desire to give God full control.

Pearls of Wisdom

The scriptural references below are biblical principles that disclose the importance of divine timing, pure motives, and the power of peace. On your dating journey, if he does not genuinely receive you, know that there is no obligation to impose greatness on anyone.

- Judges 16:16 - *And when it came to pass, when she pestered him daily with her words and pressed him, so his soul was vexed to death.*

  Delilah received what she pressured Sampson for, but she did not get his heart. We can press a man to *be* and *do*, but we cannot pressure true love from his heart. The story of Sampson and Delilah is a true example of how manipulation can get you what you want, but never what you need.

- Proverbs 18:22 - *He who finds a wife finds a good thing and obtains favor from the Lord.*

  You were not created to place unmerited pressure upon a man. Continue being the "good thing" God created you to be, allow the man to pursue you without manipulation, and receive the unadulterated love that you deserve.

- I John 4:18 - *There is no fear in love, but perfect love casts out fear, because fear involves torment. But he who fears has not been made perfect in love.*

  It is the spirit of fear that causes many to force situations that God has not approved. Be so filled with love that you never fear not being loved.

- Matthew 10:14 - *And whoever will not receive you nor hear your words, when you depart from that house or city, shake the dust off your feet.*

  This principle suggests that you do not have to force the Word of God upon anyone. Similarly, on your dating journey, if a man does not genuinely receive you, you are not obligated to impose greatness upon him.

Pearl Reflection

Use the space below to reflect on the "No Pressure Zone" topic. Explain how you will use this information to Protect Your Pearls.

Pearl Affirmation:

I OWE MYSELF ENOUGH LOVE THAT THE LACK THEREOF WILL NEVER UNDERMINE MY ADMIRATION TOWARDS ME.

Pearlbits

I am so enraptured to provide some tidbits (or what I'd like to call "Pearlbits") that encouraged and empowered me as I dated and waited. Sometimes you will need something quick and simple to awaken to your worth and destroy the fearful mindset that causes you to settle. Wisdom is key to a successful, productive journey.

The Pearlbits you will read below should help you maintain confidence, consistency and character. As you receive these statements, settle within yourself that you can never draw conclusions about who a person is based on *your* desires, but by who they reveal themselves to be.

The Pearlbits can unveil games the enemy will play with our minds. We will no longer remain ignorant to his devices while they manifest through others.

It is my hope that you digest these impactful bits, and never thirst for something that was designed to drain you and not sustain you. When you embrace wisdom, you carry the tool that can prevent fatal relational errors.

Are you ready for the full exposure? Okay! Here we go!

- *No one will ever love me as he does.* Someone has already loved you more than him—Jesus.
- When he texts you "WYD" with no productive plans, text back "PYP - Protecting My Pearls."
- Never give a man the power to choose between you and her. Always chose *you* enough not to compete for any relational positions.
- *All my family and friends love him.* But has God chosen him?
- A man staying in a relationship with you is never guaranteed, but you will continually remain in a relationship with yourself.
- *What will people say if I don't make this relationship work?* What are you going to think of yourself if you settle?
- Disappointment would not be so challenging if high expectations were reserved for people with integrity.
- *If he is not the one, why won't God remove him from my life?* Because God has given *you* the power to make that decision.
- *He hurt me so badly, I don't think I can ever love again.* Do not give an ex-partner your power.
- Women who embrace the diabolical idea that a man being too nice means the relationship will not succeed, rejects what she deserves. She is still dealing with what she hates.
- Choose God's principles every time and you will see exactly where you stand with man.
- *He said he was sorry!* Sorry is a good gesture, but only repentance delivers change.

- Do not be so tucked away that the man God has for you gets lost trying to find you.
- Beware of the man who will feed your flesh but is incapable of providing for your soul.
- *I feel so alone with him.* Sis, if his presence drains your peace and taints your soul, being alone is what's keeping you sane.
- Lust cannot be satisfied, only cast out.
- Weddings are beautiful, but do not pursue the best wedding of the year and sacrifice the best marriage of a lifetime.
- Consensual sex does not equate to a consensual commitment.
- You can replace anything except *you*. Do not settle for what is beneath your worth.
- He does not have to be perfect, but he should be willing to grow.
- While you forgive others, do not forget to forgive *you*.
- If he's having a difficult time making up his mind about you, make yours up about him.
- When you lend yourself to people who do not understand value, you will begin to second-guess your worth.
- Do not ever stand yourself up; show up every time.
- Never follow any man who tells you "God will understand."
- You are the Pearl. Let him pursue you!
- Interest opens the door, but there are more important steps to take before it is sealed.
- If he lacks consistency, you will always wonder where you stand.
- Sometimes you must pull out your bible to see if the relationship aligns with scripture.

- What you allow will become the standard.
- A sharpened spirit will help you see that which your natural eyes cannot.
- "No" is a complete sentence. The moment you must defend your values is a sign of being unequally yoked.
- You may not agree on some things, but the relationship will not be productive if you do not agree on the important things.
- He took for granted how much you loved *you* until you left him.
- He shows you clear signs of disinterest each time he undermines you.
- If he *is* the one, do not allow your past, insecurities, or the influences around you to push him away.
- You can date *and* maintain high standards.
- You are the Pearl. Allow him the time to find you.
- STOP looking for a verbal, "I do not want you." He expresses it every time he undermines the value of your Pearls.
- It is wise and necessary to discuss sexual expectations before marriage.
- The Pearl Trade replaced the Pearl with oil. However, the replacement did not take any value from the Pearl!
- Do not allow unsacred acts to disrupt your power.
- Sometimes "goodbye" is all the closure you need.
- If he does not fully support the call on your life, he will eventually cause you to doubt it.
- Every productive relationship starts with first being whole.
- I do not care if you marry the most handsome man or not; his value will go up when he finds his good thing.
- Your preparation will not prevent disappointment, but it will assist you with dealing with it productively.

- Growth takes mindset adjustments, not a man.
- It will take more than extrinsic things to sustain a purposeful relationship.
- If he can have sex with you and undermine your soul, you can say "no" and not care if he leaves.
- Never place anyone higher than God.
- Building a relationship without God is like attempting to drive without a steering wheel.
- You are at risk of obtaining more holes in your soul when you look to man to fill them.
- There is nothing like a woman who refuses to settle until she has God's best.
- Where there is pain, the enemy provides deadly solutions.

Pearls of Wisdom

The scriptural references below are biblical principles that disclose the importance of allowing wisdom to be your best friend. Fear of being alone or losing someone can cloud our judgment and cause us to be reactive, and not proactive. When we demote the things that should not have the power seat in our lives and allow wisdom to be our guide, we open the door for optimum results.

- Proverbs 16:16 - *How much better to get wisdom than gold! And to get understanding is to be chosen rather than silver.*
- Proverbs 9:10 - *The fear of the Lord is the beginning of wisdom, and the knowledge of the Holy Spirit is understanding.*
- James 1:5 - *If any of you lack wisdom, let him ask of God who gives to all liberally and without reproach, and it will be given to him.*
- Proverbs 13:10 - *By pride comes nothing but strife, but with the well-advised is wisdom.*

On your dating or waiting journey, take advantage of Godly advisors. Other people's experiences and insights could be the saving grace you need to cultivate a meaningful relationship or offer the necessary wisdom to disconnect.

Pearl Reflection

Use the space below to reflect on the "Pearlbits" topic. Explain how you will use this information to Protect Your Pearls.

Pearl Affirmation:

I SEEK GOD DAILY FOR WISDOM. WITHOUT IT, I AM JOURNEYING WITHOUT DIRECTION.

Pearl Moment:

YOU ARE TOO TREASURABLE TO BE DISCOUNTED.

T. HARRIS

A Lived Experience: Deal or No Deal

I view myself as the ultimate bargain shopper. I live for finding high-quality products at nominal prices. As a matter of fact, some of my greatest conversation starters stem from bargains I have received. Most individuals, especially in these times, would delight in a deal just to splurge on other things.

There are rules to bargain shopping and walking away with the ultimate deal. When I shop, my first stop is the sales rack. Now, if you are void of patience, you would be paying full price. I very seldom buy an item simply because I see it. I can wait a full-price item out! My negotiating skills are not too shabby, either.

I recall buying my first new car when I was 21 years old. I had a trade-in vehicle, and my mom gave me a check for $10,000. She said, "If this does not buy it, it will not get bought."

I anxiously headed to the dealership. The car I wanted had 12,000 miles and was $14,000. My trade was worth maybe $1000, so you can understand my dilemma if you do the math. The salesman tried all he could to change my mind about the vehicle or talk my mom into spending more money.

As I stood in the hallway and pleaded my case, the general manager passed me. He turned my way and asked, "What do you need, darling?"

I explained that I needed him to take $4,000 off the vehicle's price so that I could purchase it and return back to college. He laughed, and the car salesman chuckled as well, but I had started the negotiation.

I showed him the check and asked, "How many people will come to this car lot with cash for this vehicle? Are you going to turn down $10,000?" By the end of the conversation, the general manager had approved my purchase of the car using only what I had. When I drove my new car to my mom's beauty salon, her mouth dropped. She just knew I would be bringing the check back and would return to school on a bus.

The psychology behind obtaining a deal entails believing you deserve it, not backing down until you get it, and having the power to walk away if it is not achievable. In life, people make deals to have money to spend on other things they find more valuable. Negotiations are not for the passive nor the impatient.

Some individuals desire brand names, even if the purchased item is inauthentic. Yes! If these consumers cannot afford the real thing, they will settle for the counterfeit. These individuals choose not to waste time waiting for sales and bargains. Ultimately, the product quality is less important than the price. Whatever an individual chooses to bargain for, or is willing to pay full price for, is a personal decision. I have settled for a cheap price over quality, and I have also paid full price with the fear of missing out on what I desired.

It is lawful and acceptable to bargain shop. It causes many to feel a sense of accomplishment when they catch a sale. However, when it comes to *you*, you are not up for bargaining. You are not a product; you are too precious to cheapen yourself to fit into another person's space. Your worth is immeasurable, but when you do not know it, or believe it, you will cut a deal with a person who will not treat you according to your worth, but according to what is easier for *him*. Just as individuals bargain for a cheaper price, you must be able to discern those who place their desires above your worth. It takes full confidence to say, "No deal!"

The pressure to leave the single zone is real. I have been there and, at times, thought it would be easier to settle than remain alone. However, when I rejected the myth that *alone* was miserable, I vowed to never shrink myself to fit into anyone's box. God has given us value through His name that we must honor and protect. We must also use wisdom before we connect with others.

I was reading a blog that mentioned Mark Ellwood, the author of *Bargain Fever: How to Shop in a Discounted World*. The blogger shared that the luxury brand Louis Vuitton only offered out-of-season products to its employees; and if any "LV" products were left over, they would burn them. Wow! Before they would risk a diminished value as a result of a price reduction, they ensured no one benefited. The brand believes in the exclusivity of its products. They will never hold sales, give public discounts, or negotiate with consumers. They are not threatened, nor do they budge with the most sophisticated bargainer. A lack of affordability or the threat of patronizing another brand does not intimidate them. They have confidence in their quality and the worth of their product.

People are attracted to quality. It gives them bragging rights, inward satisfaction, and the enjoyment of product longevity. We are not products, but we can learn a thing or two from how businesses maintain quality by not undermining its worth because of a consumer's inability to afford it.

It is in your best interest to not allow the pressures of the world to create a sense of desperation and influence you to settle for less. Certain deals were completely off my dating table—personal values I had to sort through before the connection could take place. When you procrastinate on setting your standards, it is easy for an individual to talk you down. Before you know it, you have given yourself to the top negotiator who has no intention to settle down with you.

I encourage you to know your nonnegotiable preferences. I would take *myself* on dates before I made a deal with someone who would taint my soul and have me on an emotional roller coaster. I could not give discounts for something that cost me so much. Becoming the me that I am today costs a lot! It was not a cheap journey to get here. The hard work, sacrifices, dedication, and so much more were quite expensive.

Walt's demonstration of love for me was not only through material things, but he saw my value and was willing to honor it. I confidently laid my non-negotiables on our dating table.

- Preaching is not a hobby for me; it is a lifestyle that I value. Before dating, I had already settled on it being my calling, and obedience to God was nonnegotiable.
- The enemy was after my life. Because he could not take me out with the divorce, he desired to finish me off with a different method. Rushing into a commitment before God gave me clear confirmation was nonnegotiable.
- My son is a top priority over my personal desires. My care and obligation to him are nonnegotiable.

- I have nieces, goddaughters, and a countless number of girls who look to me as a role model. Just as it was a non-negotiable for my son to see or experience me in a noncommitted relationship, I honored those girls in the same manner.
- Growing together in God, life, and love was non-negotiable.
- I understand how pride causes many people and relationships to fail. Perfection was not required, but character and the willingness to evolve spiritually were non-negotiable.

These are just a few nonnegotiable preferences that weeded many people out. It is possible that they were *good* but not fitting for me. Walt did not attempt to bargain with me on the important issues. It was not because he was desperate and did not want to lose me; it was because he knew I was worth it. A non-negotiable may be a dealbreaker for one who is too cheap to invest, but rest assured, the *right* one is willing to pay full price, plus tax.

As you spend time with yourself, it may be beneficial to conduct a reassessment of your worth. Sometimes "struggle dating" or excessive waiting occurs because you have allowed life's happenings, insecurities, or the rush to change your single status to influence you to place yourself in a market where there are only takers, and a lack of investors. People make deals out of fear and anxiousness, only to find themselves with spiritual, emotional, and mental debt.

Christ did not cut any deals for our souls. He desired to be reconciled with us and paid the ultimate price with his life. When you ponder the act of true love, my hope is that you never make a deal with a man whose goal is to destroy your soul. As you consider your worth and destroy any discounts you have displayed to bargain-daters, understand that any good investor looks for a return. I would be remiss to omit the fact that the one God sends you is just as worthy. If he is willing to pay full price with his life, commitment, and love, it is only reasonable for you to position yourself to do the same.

As I dated Walt, I did not discount myself, and neither did he. We were both willing to give and take whatever was appropriate to be together. It required transparency about past situations and the ability to expose our authentic selves, which gave us the clarity we needed to choose to invest or not. When a person knows what they are truly receiving, risks and all, it is easier to make a conscious decision and commit to it. We both desired to pay full price because the gains we acquired by having each other outweighed the risk of not being together.

Pearls of Wisdom

The scriptural references below are biblical principles that disclose the importance of investment, sacrifice, and commitment. As you date, observe the existence of the model provided through Christ. Where there are no genuine and meaningful sacrifices, there are fewer chances for consistency and commitment.

- I John 3:16 - *By this we know love because He laid down His life for us. And we also ought to lay down our lives for the brethren.*
- Matthew 13:45-46 - *Again the kingdom of heaven is like a merchant seeking beautiful pearls, who, when he had found one pearl of great price, went and sold all that he had and bought it.*
- I Corinthians 7:23 - *You were bought at a price; do not become slaves of men.*
- John 3:16 - *For God so loved the world that He gave His only begotten son, that whoever believes in Him should not perish but have everlasting life.*
- Isaiah 53:5 - *But He was wounded for our transgressions, He was bruised for our iniquities, the chastisement for our peace was upon Him, And by His stripes we are healed.*
- Ephesians 5:25 - *Husbands, love your wives, just as Christ also loved the church and gave Himself for her.*

Pearl Reflection

Use the space below to reflect on the "Deal or No Deal" topic. Explain how you will use this information to Protect Your Pearls.

Pearl Affirmation:

I AM WORTHY OF LOVE,
BUT I WILL NOT LOWER MY
VALUE TO OBTAIN IT.

Pearl Moment:

TAKE YOUR TIME BUILDING; NOTHING OF VALUE IS BUILT INSTANTANEOUSLY.

T. HARRIS

A Lived Experience: The Building Process

When I was a little girl, one of my favorite books was *The Three Little Pigs*. I will not assume you know the story, so I will give you a quick synopsis.

In this fable, there are three little pigs who use three different materials to build their houses. From my understanding, each pig was encouraged to build a house because their mom could no longer take care of them.

Each pig had the same opportunity, but hugely different mindsets. The story reveals how one built his home with a lazy mindset. He wanted to get the work done quickly because he did not want to work at all. So, he built his house with straw.

The second pig was second-level lazy and went a little further to build his house with sticks. They both wanted to play more than work, and they undermined the value of hard work, dedication, and commitment. The third pig's mindset was goals. Of all the available materials, he chose to build his home with brick. It would offer substantial protection.

While the other two pigs were finished, the third was still building. The two of them played and enjoyed themselves, but their actions did not interrupt the third pig's focus. He kept building as they played. Not even their celebrating could make him jealous or rush his process so that he could join in with them. He knew what he wanted, and he was not going to shortchange himself. He desired a different outcome and was willing to dedicate his time to do the work.

One day, a wolf came through with a vengeance, but the third pig's house was sturdy and looked as if it could handle strong winds brought upon them by the wolf. When the pig-hungry wolf came near, he blew down the houses made of straw and sticks. Thankfully, the two pigs got away and took refuge in the brick house of the third pig. The wolf followed, but he did not receive the same outcome. No matter how many times he huffed and puffed, the house was still standing. His persistence was not successful because the house was protected!

The substance we use as we build is essential to the end product. It has been shared many times that the process of building a home begins long before the foundation is poured. When you look at the finished product of a dream home, know that its existence required much work and preparation.

There are certain steps everyone must implement no matter the cost of the structure. You can have the best plan and the finances to back it, but if those plans are not approved, your dream home will never become a reality. This is also the reality of a dream relationship. All productive building takes time, needs approval, and requires quality material. Whatever you invest into it is what you will get out of it. If you allow anything to rush your relationship-building process, fail to implement quality substance, or fail to build with the right partner, the structure will be at a high risk of collapsing.

Imagine if you moved into your supposed dream home, and you discovered that because of time limitations, no roof was provided. Just as you would obtain a checklist for the structural requirements of a building, it is imperative to do the same for relationship-building.

It is so easy to look at everyone's dating journey and observe their fun and underestimate the importance of your building process. I, too, endured the ache of viewing beautiful pictures. However, I was like the third pig. I was done with quick fixes, and I desired productivity over playing games.

The moment I knew that Walt was deeply committed to Christ, I was willing to start our building process. All homes, no matter how large or small, must have a foundation. As a part of our relationship-building process, we agreed that Christ would be our foundation. We understood that His foundation would uphold us through any season or storm.

Throughout our process, it was important that we communicated our personal ideas for the relationship, were equally invested, and were prepared to pass spiritual inspections on issues that could jeopardize our permit to be together. I shared, he shared, and we evaluated what we could or could not tolerate. Thank God we mutually agreed that our pros outweighed the cons, and we passed inspection.

However, we were not comfortable with opening up to others and decided not to allow many people in during our building process. It was not because of a lack of love for them, but our focus, and most importantly, hearing from God, took presidency. The more access individuals have to your building process before completion, the more opinions, perspectives, and pressures there will be to blur your vision, overwhelm your ideas and sometimes cause confusion in the relationship. We had a small, yet powerful, number of people who were a part of our dating circle that desired God's will for our lives and to see us happy.

One of the questions that I am asked most is: What if you take time to build a relationship, and it is still destroyed? There are risks involved with building anything, but having insurance brings peace of mind in the event that damage occurs. When two people decide to build together, life can come at the relational structure quite hard. It is important to understand that nothing ensures our heart more than the One who created it.

It cannot be promised that any relational structure will last forever; but when the right process is implemented, the risk of destruction decreases. In any event, where relational damage occurs, the most important concept of Protecting Your Pearls is to never lose the one pearl that is irreplaceable, and that is you.

Pearls of Wisdom

The scriptural references below are biblical principles that disclose the importance of productive relationship-building and the materials needed to ensure a successful outcome. As you date or wait, consider the importance of proper planning, having a strong foundation, and the substance with which you choose to build.

- Psalm 127:1 - *Unless the Lord builds the house, they labor in vain who built it, Unless the Lord guards the city, the watchman stays awake in vain.*
- Matthew 21:42 - *Jesus said to them, "Have you never read in the Scriptures: 'The stone which the builders rejected has become the chief cornerstone. This was the Lord's doing, and it is marvelous in our eyes'?"*
- Galatians 5:22-23 - *But the fruit of the Spirit is love, joy, peace, longsuffering, kindness, goodness, faithfulness, gentleness, self-control. Against such there is no law.*
- Proverbs 24:3 - *Through wisdom a house is built, and by understanding it is established; And by knowledge the rooms are filled with all precious and pleasant riches.*

Pearl Reflection

Use the space below to reflect on the "The Building Process" topic. Explain how you will use this information to Protect Your Pearls.

Pearl Affirmation:

AS MUCH AS I DESIRE TO HAVE A DREAM RELATIONSHIP WITH HIM, I WILL FOCUS MORE ON BUILDING MY DREAM RELATIONSHIP WITH GOD.

Pearl Moment:

THERE IS NOTHING MORE BEAUTIFUL THAN SEEING A WOMAN WHO IS COGNIZANT OF THE REALITY THAT SHE MATTERS.

T. HARRIS

A Lived Experience: You Matter!

As enthusiastic as I was to love again, it was how I loved *me* that would contribute to the success or demise of me and Walt's relationship. The long conversations, making plans for our future, visits, and all the spiritual connectedness we experienced were indeed an answered prayer. Despite everything I wanted prior to my dream relationship, I loved *myself* enough to wait.

How we balance our individuality is one of the keys to our relational success. Many times, we abandon ourselves and all that pertains to us to stay connected to an individual. The man that is for you will understand that self-care would benefit him in every way that he is connected to you. As for myself, I have been in ministry for close to 20 years. I am a business owner, author, talk show host, and most importantly, I am a mom. I learned many years ago that when you depend on others to celebrate or validate you, your healing process is ten times more difficult once disappointment creeps in, intentionally or unintentionally.

My personal experience with self-validation and self-celebration gave me leverage in each of my relationships. I established a routine to date myself for many years. I took myself to dinners and outings, including out-of-town trips. It was critical for me to love *me* as God desires. I was convinced that I mattered to Walt because he spoiled me spiritually and naturally. His respect, sacrifice, transparency, and attentiveness were abundant and served as confirmation. His imperfections were so easy to deal with because I consistently received the best of him. His heart was in a pure place, and he was humble enough to repent. I embraced the love from Walt, but not even his love was more important than the love I have for myself.

I recall a beautiful young lady who had experienced a breakup and was contemplating suicide. She sent me a direct message and asked for prayer and a quick conversation. She shared that her boyfriend of five years cheated on her multiple times, and he finally left her for another woman. Her expression of humiliation and disappointment transitioned to negative self-talk and self-blame. What concerned me was not the hurt she experienced, but her inability to sense enough self-importance that another fallible being could cause her to question her very existence. When the person she decided to be with undermined her, she began to undermine herself.

I shared the reality that many married and single women suffer despair due to the actions of those who promised to love them. Somehow, because of this promise, it is easy to desire him so much that you take less care of yourself, miss or ignore red flags, and then end up so unbearably hurt that life seems unlivable. The good news is that perspectives can change, and you can begin to see yourself as the Pearl God created you to be. When serving, being a great mom, dating, or getting married to the love of your life, do not allow dust to cover your own pearls while you are shining others'.

Individuals protect things. If they lose, or do not have, the ability to do so, they invest in protection. In case the protective investment fails, they obtain insurance to, at the very least, be reimbursed the value of the lost item.

Why does a person go through the trouble to protect what will eventually lose value, break, or be stolen? What we protect is dear to our hearts. You are the dearest, and because you matter, I urge you to put a protective plan in place.

When you are cognizant that *you* matter to you, it will be virtually impossible for you to lose *yourself* in the process of someone leaving. After my divorce, I had to recognize that I mattered with or without that individual in my life. I set a healthy pattern of clinging to *me* by nurturing the personal relationship I had with myself.

I want to say this again: you matter! The way you love yourself will impact the love you give, and the treatment you accept from others. Be encouraged to Protect Your Pearls because everything connected to them will benefit.

One thing that emerged when I began to matter to *me* is what I accepted. When my expectations, values, and self-worth were imbalanced, people with the wrong motives easily had an advantage over me. Well, of course! There were moments when I had to regroup and put myself in the proper place again, and again—as many times necessary. As I continued my "I matter" journey, I did not become selfish. It was always important to value others as I liked to be valued. I just refused to be discounted.

The Bible story in John 4:4-26 is about a lady who was about to lose herself because of society's systems, promiscuity, and religion. She was not privy to what she needed; rituals that made her feel accepted undermined the authentic relationship she needed with God. It was easy to get lost in what could not keep her yet constantly drain her worth.

She was excommunicated because of her lifestyle. Daily, she would draw water at a time when no one else was there. One day, she approached the well and Jesus stood beside it. He asked her for a drink, and she was appalled that he, a Jew, had asked for something. Her religious mindset almost cost her the wholeness God was offering. Jews looked down on Samaritans, but Jesus saw her as His.

As Jesus spoke with her, he exposed the things that quenched her value in her own eyes. She eventually opened up to him and confirmed that his words were true. He offered her a different type of thirst-quencher—living water. Living water gave her the power to live for God and to see herself as He saw her. Sin and tradition no longer had the power to prevent her from embracing God's love, her purpose, and every ounce of her worth. Though she may not have mattered to many, she mattered to Him, and eventually, to herself. It was an amazing wonder; she went from being shunned by an entire community to bringing them to the knowledge of Christ. Remarkable things happen when we understand just how much we matter.

We cannot control people. They tend to do what they desire to do no matter how much we pressure or love them. It is just the reality of dealing with people. We must be prepared for what the relationship produces, and sometimes it is beyond our control. Most people do not set out to hurt others. It is gracious to leave room for immaturity, negative life experiences, and a lack of self-control.

We get caught in the crossfire a lot of times, but it is not the crossfire that can make or break us; it is how we deal with the crossfire, or if we even allow the crossfire to affect us, that matters most. Therefore, it is imperative that you matter to *you* because it is not promised or written in stone that you will matter to him forever. So, even as a married woman, I still find time for just me. I still celebrate *me*. I still uphold my value system. I still have expectations and standards. I still look beautiful for *me* first. I still treat myself with great worth and respect. I will never undermine the need of *me* to me!

When you matter to yourself, you are positioned for the win to manifest. Your goals are executed. Your purpose is not put on the shelf. Your faith is not undermined. Your dreams are still a priority. You will refuse to lower your integrity when someone's inability, or refusal, to love you is made known. And because you matter to *you*, you leave a little wiggle room in every relationship—just in case you may need to slip out.

My "I Matter" Protective Plan consists of the following:

- I matter, so God's sovereignty and will for my life matters.
- I matter, so red flags matter.
- I matter, so diabolical negotiations are not entertained.
- I matter, so I depend on God for the hydration only He can give.
- I matter, so being equally yoked matters.
- I matter, so back shelves are needed for items, and not for me.
- I matter, so I take my time to evaluate those who desire to be with me.
- I matter, so I mark the entrance and exit in every relationship.
- I matter, so every person connected to me matters.
- I matter, so my purpose and every soul that is assigned to me matters.
- I matter, so my accomplishments and goals matter.

- I matter, so my mindset matters.
- I matter, so my peace matters.
- I matter, so I empower others to know that they matter.
- I matter, so I am most intrigued by the intrinsic and not the extrinsic.

Pearls of Wisdom

The scriptural references below are biblical principles that disclose the importance of *you*! You mattered so much to God that He refused to remain in eternity without giving you the opportunity to join Him. Your significance to *you* is the window through which you determine who to let in and who to keep out.

- Luke 12:6-7 - *Are not five sparrows sold for two copper coins? And not one of them is forgotten before God. But the very hairs on your head are all numbered. Do not fear; therefore, you are of more value than many sparrows.* (You matter!)
- Luke 15:4-7 - *What man of you, having a hundred sheep, if he loses one of them, does not leave the ninety-nine in the wilderness, and go after the one which is lost until he finds it? And when he has found it, he lays it on his shoulders, rejoicing. And when he comes home, he calls together his friends and neighbors, saying to them. 'Rejoice with me, for I have found which was lost!' I say to you that likewise there will be more joy in heaven over one sinner who repents than ninety-nine just persons who need no repentance.* (You matter!)
- Romans 5:8 - *But God demonstrates His own love toward us, in that while we were still sinners, Christ died for us.* (You matter!)

Pearl Affirmation:

I MATTER! I BELIEVE IT, AND IT WILL SHOW IN THE WAY THAT I LOVE GOD AND MYSELF, IN MY TREATMENT OF OTHERS, AND IN HOW I ALLOW OTHERS TO TREAT ME.

Pearl Moment:

CREATE A PERSONAL QUOTE ABOUT LOVE.

A Lived Experience: He Loves Me, or So I Thought

I remember playing the "He Loves Me Not" game growing up, hoping as I pulled the flower petals that Tevin Campbell would call me. Ha! As I grew older, I realized the song "Can We Talk" was not intended for me.

There are many games that people enjoy playing. I strongly believe that games can destress, create healthy competition and add a bit of flair to one's life. However, playing the game of love is awfully risky and can bring trauma to relationships and people. For the sake of your wellbeing, it is very irresponsible to continue in naivety. There is a special knowing that is a part of our natural build. When we are not clear about how someone feels about us, we should hold back the best parts of us until we know for sure.

I get it! I have been played multiple times, but subconsciously I already knew it. Because I connected too soon, it was particularly challenging to act on it. My grandmother, Gloria, calls it "love blind" when we become so blind that we cannot see it is *not* love.

In many relationships, love seals the deal too quickly. When love is not fully understood, it is easy to mistake one form of love for another. As a result, many find themselves stuck in toxic situations and are begging God to get them out but will not take the necessary action with the power God provides. I know firsthand.

Love is incredibly special; it creates bonds and connections that are indescribable. I remember the first time Walt and I declared our love for each other. It was so special, pure, and mutual—and different than anything I had experienced in previous relationships because of the love I had for myself. I was completely open to receive the love he had for me because I deserve it, and I am worth it. The difference-maker was that he not only spoke it—he also showed it.

When someone tells my son's grandmother, whom we call "Poo Doo", that she's loved, her main response is "love is what it does."

When I think about the true essence of love, I think about the conversation Jesus had with Peter in John 21:17.

> *The third time he said to him, "Simon son of John, do you love me?"*
>
> *Peter was hurt because Jesus asked him the third time, "Do you love me?" He said, "Lord, you know all things; you know that I love you."*
>
> *Jesus said, "Feed my sheep."*

The word *love* in this passage carries the connotation of phileo, which means to be fond of or to be a friend. I considered this scripture because I understood the three types of love and the many people who misappropriate them all.

- Phileo - the love of a friend.
- Eros - a love that stems from romance, physical attraction, and touches.
- Agape - the love that exceeds situations and circumstances. A love that is demonstrated by God, an unfailing love.

The longevity of any relationship will depend upon the type of love commitment that has taken root. It was especially important for us to genuinely love each other without sexual ties because eros is blinding and dangerous to enter into without a covenant. If Walt could be a good friend, grow more in love with Christ, and hold himself to a Godly standard, I knew he would be able to love me for the long haul. When we depend upon the eros type of love to solidify a relationship, we set ourselves up for failure in every area of our lives, especially spiritually.

Protecting My Pearls meant that I had to be much more than a snuggle-buddy, romantic night, or the object of physical attraction. In today's time, social pressures have caused women to reject the sacredness of their sexuality, and there are spiritual and natural consequences that come with the belief that sex equals love. However, when shortcomings manifest, when obstacles knock at your relational door, and when distractions kick your door in, it will take more than romance to keep your relationship going.

During my first outing with him, I felt that Walt was capable of sweeping me off my feet. He was, and is, a perfect gentleman! The decision to not go on a date or see him for five months, as I previously mentioned, allowed us to build a more genuine bond that did not stem from romance but would eventually blossom into it. For me, partnering on spiritual growth was the new image of relational flair. We grew into a love that caused us to honor, respect, and spiritually empower each other.

I remember having a dream that he was not telling me something, and I was very direct about the dream. I shared the details of the dream with him, and he became totally transparent. Eros, the love that stems from touches and romance, sometimes blurs discernment. Had I, or we, placed eros before phileo, we would have been more in tune with our emotional senses, versus our spiritual awakening.

At every point before our covenant agreement, I was willing to love him from afar if I learned that he was not coming from a pure place. So many people have given themselves to dangerous relational bonds in the name of love. If it undermines the call on your life, undermines the God in your life, or takes you away from *you*, that love should be reevaluated. The feelings can remain, but it is to your detriment if *you* remain.

I remember a time when I just knew I was in love—and stayed in the name of love. I fought for the relationship in the name of love; I took, and took again, what God did not require of me in the name of love. So, I get it! The feeling is so overwhelming that it causes many to believe it has filled the voids in their lives. After the relationship ended, I concluded that true love would have strengthened me to walk away. I committed from that moment on that being told I was loved would not dismiss responsibility, accountability, or action.

Countless women are abused, cheated on, taken advantage of, and stay because of the love they feel for a person, and they dismiss the fact that their love is not being reciprocated. Recognizing this pattern prior to marriage is essential and is a part of your relational responsibility. It is easier to break up than it is to get a divorce. When I remarried, I wanted to alleviate every avenue of divorce within my power, and not allowing love to complete or undermine other qualities assisted me with understanding my partner.

- "But I love him" will not change him. That is his responsibility.

- "But I love him" will not make him genuinely love you. That is his responsibility.
- "But I love him" will not keep him from seeing other people. That is his responsibility.
- "But I love him" will not seal the deal, and that is something you must acknowledge and be courageous enough to confront.

When love is tested, whatever type of love you settled for will manifest. Even now, I receive many messages along these lines: "You mean to tell us, love did not seal it?" No! Love was a great bonus. It deeply depended upon the type of love that was manifesting.

My final confirmation that our love signified a lasting bond was when I felt that he would sacrifice even himself for me. I felt safe, provided for, and top priority.

Let us leave the "if he loves me or not" for the games. In reality, you deserve to be loved, adored, and cherished, and God has given you a special inner-tool to discern it: the Holy Spirit.

Pearls of Wisdom

In the space provided below, list scriptural references and biblical principles that describe the importance of genuine love, and the precautions one should take on the journey to finding it.

Pearl Affirmation:

CREATE A PERSONAL AFFIRMATION ABOUT THE LOVE YOU DESERVE.

Pearl Moment:

A PEARL IS STILL A PEARL NO MATTER HOW MUCH MUD IS ON IT.

T. HARRIS

Wash Your Pearls, Girly

You did it, and I am so proud of you! I am almost positive that during the process of reading this guide, distractions came from numerous directions. Maybe you placed this guide down from time to time, got busy, or felt tempted to do things your way. No matter the distraction or setback, you made it to the victorious ending!

My prayer is that the content provided in this guide empowers you to see the power and purpose of dating God's way and to see and love yourself no less than God does. I am so excited about your continued journey. My declaration is that you will not have to search for love, compromise, or plead and that someone who is worthy of you, and you of him, will be easily sniffed out by the anointing of God!

Now it is time for the washing, and I mean that literally. When I began to post about Protect Your Pearls, I received many messages and calls, which confirmed that many single and married women felt they had not properly protected their Pearls.

The message that sparked my determination to encourage and empower as many women as I could with the P.Y.P. teachings was from a beautiful, intelligent, and kind woman. She asked what I meant by "Protect Your Pearls". Her personal reflection of herself was that she was fearless. Her life experiences, choices, and how she saw herself convinced her that she had destroyed her Pearls. I shared the synopsis of this guide with her, and she realized that every Pearl experience gave her power. I explained how my ability and platform would demonstrate how Pearls may get lost, trampled over, attacked, and undermined, but are priceless and will never lose their value. She wept to learn that, after all this time, she too has Pearls, and that her life's triumphs or hiccups did not disqualify her, nor could deny her.

- Ask for forgiveness.

  John 1:9 says…

  If we confess our sins, He is faithful and just to forgive us our sins and cleanse us from all unrighteousness.

  The first step to washing your Pearls is to acknowledge that you have not been as careful to protect them as you should have, and then express your need for forgiveness. It is the blood of Jesus that does the cleansing!

- Forgive.

  Matthew 6:15, says…

  But if you do not forgive men their trespasses, neither will your Father forgive your trespasses. Just as willing as you are to receive forgiveness, it is essential that you render it.

- Be wise with your Pearls.

  Matthew 7:6 says…

  Do not give what is holy to dogs, and do not cast your pearls before swine, lest they trample them under their feet, and turn and tear you to pieces.

Be reminded that pig mentalities do not recognize, honor, nor can be privy to what has value. Now is the time to go into every spiritual pigsty and get your Pearls back courageously and intentionally.

Here is a bonus! The next time you shower, as the water hits you and you are washing the oils and dirt build-up from your body, declare this:

As I wash my body, I wash my soul of every evil connection and demonic tie. I wash my mind of negativity. As I cleanse my ears, I flush out every arbitrary voice and ask God to give me ears to hear. If my hands have sinned against God, I pray as David did for clean hands and a pure heart. As I wash my feet, I surrender my steps to the Lord. I place my Pearls, and everything that pertains to me and will ultimately give God the glory, around my neck and claim Jesus as the clamp that holds it together.

Continue this journey in patience, love, and wisdom; and have fun as you date or wait.

Pearl Affirmation:

I'VE GOT THIS WITH GOD.

It's Time to Journal Your Dating Journey

You have made it through the content. I hope you are inspired to take action and apply the things that will make your dating or waiting journey a lifetime experience. Please use the Protect Your Pearls journal prompts to assist you with developing your ideas, desires, and standards for dating differently. Read each prompt and elaborate on each point as much as you can. These prompts will give you a cue to spark your very own dating guidelines, expectations and expand your perspective. I encourage you to write daily or as you experience your journey.

Date ______________

Protect Your Pearls Journal Prompts

How important is it for you to make yourself happy? What are some daily self-care rituals you implement, and what can you add to this list?

Date ______________

Protect Your Pearls Journal Prompts

What are some ideal scriptures that can encourage you on the days you are experiencing the dating or waiting blues?

Date ______________

Protect Your Pearls Journal Prompts

What are some walls from your past that prevent you from being genuinely open to dating and being loved?

Date ______________

Protect Your Pearls Journal Prompts

What is that one song that can relieve, get you going, and cause you to dance? Why this song?

Date ______________

Protect Your Pearls Journal Prompts

What are the top 3-10 things you are most grateful for during your dating or waiting journey? What is it about these things that make you grateful?

Date ______________

Protect Your Pearls Journal Prompts

What are some things you are doing to prepare for love during your dating or waiting experience? How do you think these things will prepare you?

Date ______________

Protect Your Pearls Journal Prompts

If you had to write a letter to your spouse (or future spouse) about the fears you face about dating or waiting, what would that letter entail?

Date ______________

Protect Your Pearls Journal Prompts

Describe the ideal date that would not leave you in a compromised position.

Date ______________

Protect Your Pearls Journal Prompts

Describe the perfect dating or waiting accountability partner. Who do you turn to, and why is it important?

Date ______________

Protect Your Pearls Journal Prompts

How have your previous dating experiences invoked change for present or future dating experiences?

Date ______________

Protect Your Pearls Journal Prompts

What has been some dating or waiting obstacles? How have you hurdled them?

Date ______________

Protect Your Pearls Journal Prompts

Tell God all about it, whatever it is, right here in this space!

Date ______________

Protect Your Pearls Journal Prompts

Who is that couple you admire the most? How could you gain insight into their relationship and establish mentorship with them?

Date ______________

Protect Your Pearls Journal Prompts

How are you honoring God during your dating or waiting experience? In what areas could you be more intentional?

Date ______________

Protect Your Pearls Journal Prompts

What are some qualities you bring to the dating table that would improve the dating experience?

Date ______________

Protect Your Pearls Journal Prompts

How are you applying the rule to being self-sufficient as you make dating connections?

Date ______________

Protect Your Pearls Journal Prompts

What resources could or have inspired you during your dating or waiting journey? Write them down and share how they have been of assistance to you.

Date _______________

Protect Your Pearls Journal Prompts

How can the one you are dating or waiting for assist you with Protecting Your Pearls?

Date ______________

Protect Your Pearls Journal Prompts

What are your top triggers when faced with relational disappointments? Create some trigger strategies that will assist you on your dating or waiting journey.

Date _______________

Protect Your Pearls Journal Prompts

In what ways have you settled because of the desired relationship? What are some strategies you can implement to minimize your willingness to settle for less?

Date ______________

Protect Your Pearls Journal Prompts

What are some tangible or intangible things you are holding on to keep the wrong person in your heart? Are you willing to let these things go so that you can move on?

Date ______________

Protect Your Pearls Journal Prompts

In what ways are you holding yourself accountable as you date or wait?

Date _______________

Protect Your Pearls Journal Prompts

Who do you blame the most for your dating failures? Why?

Date ______________

Protect Your Pearls Journal Prompts

What are some daily personal habits that you can create to make yourself great?

Date ______________

Protect Your Pearls Journal Prompts

Would you date yourself? Why or why not?

Date ______________

Protect Your Pearls Journal Prompts

What is your dating exit plan just in case things don't work?

Date ______________

Protect Your Pearls Journal Prompts

Give yourself a pep talk as you would give to a friend:

Date _______________

Protect Your Pearls Journal Prompts

What are some things or people you have avoided or abandoned during your dating or waiting experience?

Date ____________

Protect Your Pearls Journal Prompts

What new godly dating experiences are you open to embracing after reading this guide?

Date _______________

Protect Your Pearls Journal Prompts

How are you Protecting Your Pearls?

Made in United States
Orlando, FL
04 October 2023

37574467R00075